Merrill Lynch is proud to sponsor *London's Monets* at the National Gallery, an exhibition that brings together, for the first time, an extraordinarily rich variety of Claude Monet's paintings, all from public and private London collections. As a seminal figure in the Impressionist movement, Monet bridged the nineteenth and twentieth centuries. So it is particularly fitting that this exhibition marks an exchange of works between the Tate Gallery and the National Gallery.

Merrill Lynch's roots in London go back nearly fifty years, and this year we are celebrating the twenty-fifth anniversary of the establishment of our London-based private bank, Merrill Lynch International Bank. As a corporate citizen of long-standing, we have benefited from London's position as one of the greatest cultural centres in the world. We, in turn, are pleased to have this opportunity to help make possible a brilliant display of art that will attract the interest both of Londoners and of visitors from around the globe.

Monet's work, revolutionary in its time, helped people to see the world in new and different ways. We hope you enjoy this splendid collection of this great artist's works.

DANIEL P. TULLY
Chairman of the Board
Merrill Lynch & Co., Inc.

DAVID H. KOMANSKY
President and Chief Executive Officer
Merrill Lynch & Co., Inc.

CHRISTOPHER REEVES
Chairman
Merrill Lynch Europe PLC

FOREWORD

What would Monet think of a Monet exhibition in the National Gallery? He knew the Gallery well of course: while in London in 1870 and 1871, to avoid the Franco-Prussian war and the miseries of the Commune, he was a frequent visitor to Trafalgar Square, and it was here that he made the crucial discovery of Turner, whose presence can be sensed ever more strongly in his later works. He would surely be pleased to have his works shown only a few rooms away from those of the British master. He knew London well, too, returning on a number of occasions to explore the colouristic possibilities offered by the city's spectacular pollution – most notably in 1901, to work on his extensive series of London pictures, exhibited in Paris in 1904.

On the other hand, he also knew that the English were reluctant to buy his pictures, and selling pictures was very important to Monet, whose increasingly expensive life-style depended on his steadily growing market success. But as the Monet boom got into its stride from the 1880s onwards, the British stood aside. While his work was being enthusiastically collected by French and American patrons – within two years of the fifteen *Grainstacks* being exhibited as a series in 1891, for example, fourteen of them had gone to the United States – it was almost impossible to find serious buyers for the pictures in England. Indeed in 1909 the National Art Collections Fund, by no means blinkered or old-fashioned in their taste, specifically declined to buy one of the late views of London which were then on the market.

Yet today, against all the odds, London is rich in Monets. As this display shows, it is possible, through the works in our public and private collections, to follow Monet's entire career across six decades, from the crystalline still life and landscape of the 1860s to the dissolving splendours of the almost final *Water-Lilies*.

The occasion for this small celebratory exhibition is the decision taken by the Trustees of the National and Tate Galleries that, for the next four years, all the continental paintings before 1900 should be shown together at the National Gallery, and those after 1900 should (with a few exceptions) hang at the Tate. Like Cézanne, Monet is clearly an artist crucial to both centuries, and so some of his post-1900 works will remain at Trafalgar Square, to show the whole range of his achievement, while the *Water-Lilies*, a type of work of great importance for developments later in twentieth-century painting, will move first to Millbank and then to Bankside – an arrangement that will, we hope, allow us to fulfil our two overlapping obligations: to do proper honour to the artist, and to tell as clearly as possible the story of European painting.

Before the new division takes place, however, we wanted to show all the Tate and National Gallery Monets together, and we have been fortunate that the Courtauld Institute Galleries have generously agreed to lend theirs, thus bringing together for the first time all the public collections of his work. It is often regretted that the London holdings of nineteenth-century artists are split; but it is always perfectly possible, through co-operative ventures like this one, to enjoy the benefits of both unity and diversity, alternately seeing the artist as a whole, and viewing him in a number of different contexts.

That our public collections now have so many Monets is a tribute to the dedication, energy and

The Thames below Westminster, detail (Plate 5)

London's Monets

KATHLEEN ADLER
JOHN LEIGHTON

National Gallery Publications, London

This book was published to accompany an exhibition at
THE NATIONAL GALLERY, LONDON
12 March – 5 May 1997

First published in Great Britain in 1997 by
National Gallery Publications Limited
5/6 Pall Mall East, London SW1Y 5BA
Reprinted 1997

ISBN 1 85709 212 0
525223

British Library Cataloguing-in-Publication Data
A catalogue record is available from the British Library

Designed by Tim Harvey
Printed and bound in Great Britain by Ashdown Press
Limited, London

Front cover: *Antibes*, detail (Plate 14)
Back cover: *Still Life* (Plate 2)

generosity of a few enlightened enthusiasts, who frequently had to confront vigorous opposition, not least from the National Gallery. In 1905, Frank Rutter, a critic who consistently championed the Impressionist cause, was determined that the nation should acquire its first Monet. Rutter accordingly launched the French Impressionist Fund to buy *Lavacourt under Snow* (known then as *Snow Effect at Vétheuil*), only to be told that the Trustees of the National Gallery would not accept a Monet, even if given. It was, it may be said in the Trustees' defence, still uncertain whether work by a living artist should enter the National Gallery, and the money was therefore used to buy *The Entrance to Trouville Harbour* by Boudin, who had safely died seven years earlier. Monet's snow scene did nonetheless wind up in the National Gallery, for it was bought subsequently by Sir Hugh Lane, and bequeathed by him to the Gallery in 1917 (when Monet was of course still alive).

But even that bequest, the foundation of the national holding of Impressionists, was not welcomed by all. One of the clearest statements of just what the admirers of the Impressionists were up against was made by Lord Redesdale, a Trustee of the National Gallery, who in 1914 opposed even the idea of a loan of such pictures: 'I should as soon expect to hear of a Mormon service being conducted in St Paul's Cathedral as to see an exhibition of the works of the modern French Art-rebels in the sacred precincts of Trafalgar Square.' Fortunately, Rutter and those who thought like him persisted and, in time, prevailed. The Courtauld gift of £50,000 to the Tate Gallery in 1923 transformed the situation and brought two great Monets – *The Beach at Trouville* and *The Water-Lily Pond* – to join the Lavacourt snow-scene.

The benefactions of Lane and Courtauld set a pattern, and, since then, the national collection of Monets has been steadily enriched by gifts and bequests, beginning with the NACF's presentation in 1926 of *Poplars on the Epte* and *Woman seated on a Bench*, and continued most recently by the bequests of *Bathers at La Grenouillère* and *The Museum at Le Havre*, and the presentation in 1996 of the early *La Pointe de la Hève* by the Corporate Benefactors of the National Gallery.

For this display, we wanted to add to the pictures now in the national collection the most distinguished works by the artist in London private collections. To our delight, the owners agreed with alacrity, and our visitors will quickly be able to see how much our view of Monet is enriched by their generosity. We are extremely grateful to them for agreeing to be separated for two months from pictures which give them great pleasure, and we hope that the response of the public will vindicate their decision. I am sure that all would want to record a special debt of gratitude to Her Majesty Queen Elizabeth, The Queen Mother for the loan of her magnificent landscape, which once belonged to Monet's great friend and supporter, Georges Clemenceau.

Another of Monet's close associates, Octave Mirbeau, argued that Monet's art could be a powerful source for social good, showing to everybody the beauties of the world which were theirs to enjoy: 'The people', he wrote, 'have a right to beauty as they have a right to bread.' Thanks to the whole-hearted support of Merrill Lynch, we are able to mount this display, and to do so without making any charge. This will, without doubt, allow a very large number of people to enjoy the beauty of these paintings, and to return to enjoy them again. Of that, Monet would have approved.

NEIL MACGREGOR
Director

1   La Pointe de la Hève, Sainte-Adresse

Oil on canvas, 41 × 73 cm
Signed and dated: 1864

London, National Gallery

In the early 1860s Monet was already an enthusiastic outdoor painter, and while his larger pictures were painted in the studio, the technique and the modest scale of this canvas suggest that it was painted in front of the subject. The view is taken from the beach at Sainte-Adresse near Monet's home town of Le Havre. The luminous late-afternoon sky and the subtle range of tones reflect the influence of his early mentors, Boudin and Jongkind, who had both painted at this site. Yet the painting bears the unmistakable stamp of Monet's artistic personality. From the delicate colours of the shingle beach to the ribbons of sunlight on the horizon, there is ample evidence of his rigorous observation.

Although the picture is signed and dated, it may have been painted as a study for a larger composition. At the Salon exhibition in 1865, Monet showed two large views of the Seine estuary, including a work now in the Kimbell Art Museum, Fort Worth, which shows the same view at low tide.

2 Still Life

Oil on canvas, 46 × 56 cm
Signed
About 1867

Private Collection

Monet explored the theme of still life at several points in his career (see Plate 13). Here the arrangement of fruit on a table-top is reminiscent of Chardin, and also of contemporary still lifes by François Bonvin. A number of Parisian art dealers specialised in this type of picture, and Monet may have hoped to find ready buyers for such works.

The pear in the basket marks the apex of a number of overlapping triangles, indicating that Monet set up the display carefully and precisely. The shapes of the large round apples are contrasted with the smaller circular shapes of the black and green grapes, and the fruits appear polished, so vivid are their highlights. In contrast to the more generalised effect of colour and atmosphere that Monet sought to achieve in his landscapes, here each element is observed and recorded as a separate entity, discrete from other parts of the painting.

3 Bathers at La Grenouillère

Oil on canvas, 73 × 92 cm
Signed and dated: 1869

London, National Gallery

During the summer of 1869, Monet and Renoir painted together at La Grenouillère, a leisure spot on the Seine just outside Paris. Monet told their friend Bazille: 'I do indeed have a dream, a painting, the bathing place at La Grenouillère, for which I've made a few bad sketches, but it remains a dream. Renoir...also wants to paint the same picture.'

This is one of the 'sketches', although it is only slightly smaller than the finished work (now lost) which was the culmination of the painting campaign. Monet appears to have worked on the spot, depicting boats and bathers with great verve and directness. The scene is bisected horizontally by a narrow wooden walkway which led to a small rounded island known as the 'camembert'. The play of light on the water, the movement of the moored rowing boats, and the barely indicated bathers in the sunlit river are captured with a minimum of detail. The group of two women and a man on the walkway clearly reveals Monet's gifts as a caricaturist – the vulgarity of the central woman's pose is rendered in a few quick brushstrokes.

4 The Beach at Trouville

Oil on canvas, 37.5 × 45.7 cm
Signed and dated: 1870

London, National Gallery

Monet married his first wife, Camille, on 28 June 1870, and soon afterwards he took his bride and their three-year-old son, Jean, to the fashionable resort of Trouville on the Normandy coast. This is one of several studies that Monet painted on the beach during that summer. Camille is shown at the left wearing a flowered hat and a pale blue and grey dress. Her companion may be the wife of Monet's painter friend Eugène Boudin.

Monet worked extremely quickly, using broad strokes of paint to suggest the transitory effects of light and atmosphere. Some areas, such as the hand of Madame Boudin, have been left unpainted so that the light grey priming plays an active role in the colour scheme. This is the quintessential outdoor painting – so much so that the surface is peppered with grains of sand blown there by the wind that Monet evokes in the flapping flag and the fast-moving clouds.

5　The Thames below Westminster

Oil on canvas, 47 × 72.5 cm
Signed and dated: 1871

London, National Gallery

Monet first came to London in 1870–1 to avoid the
Franco-Prussian War. He painted several memorable
pictures of the Thames, including this view looking
towards the Palace of Westminster. St Thomas's Hospital
is just visible through the mist at the far left, behind
Westminster Bridge. In the foreground the builders appear
to be working on the construction of part of the new
Victoria Embankment, or perhaps the Admiralty steps.

Monet is known to have admired Turner, whose works

he would have seen at the National Gallery. However, the
style and composition of this work relate more closely to
Japanese art and perhaps even to Whistler's simplified
views of London shrouded in mist.

The artist returned to London several times later in his
career and the Thames with the Palace of Westminster
became one of his favoured subjects.

6 The Petit Bras of the Seine at Argenteuil

Oil on canvas, 52.6 × 71.8 cm
Signed
1872

London, National Gallery

After his year of voluntary exile in England and Holland, Monet returned to France late in 1871. He settled in Argenteuil, a small suburban town on the Seine about nine kilometres from Paris. Monet's views of boats and bridges at Argenteuil are among his best-known works. In this picture, however, he has turned his back on the activity of the Seine to paint a tranquil backwater called the Petit Bras. As the name implies, this was a narrow stretch of water, separated from the main river by the Ile Marante, which is shown on the right of the picture.

The gentle mood and the traditional composition recall earlier river scenes by Daubigny and Corot. But although the overall effect of the painting is subdued, Monet achieved his greys and browns with complex mixtures of strong, clear colours. The picture seems less daring than works like *Bathers at La Grenouillère* (Plate 3), yet the artist is still preoccupied with rendering the luminosity of outdoor light.

It seems safe to assume that Monet painted this work with an eye to a commercial sale. Although his technique was innovatory, the result was sufficiently conventional to conform to an established market for modest landscapes.

7 The Museum at Le Havre

Oil on canvas, 75 × 100 cm
Signed and dated: 1873

London, National Gallery

Monet lived at Argenteuil, near Paris, from the end of 1871 until 1877, but he made occasional visits back to his home town of Le Havre. In 1873, and again in 1874, he painted views of the harbour at Le Havre, including the famous *Impression: Sunrise*, the picture from which the Impressionist movement later derived its name.

The view in this painting is taken from one of the walls of the inner harbour looking across to the Musée des Beaux-Arts. This building was destroyed during the Second World War and has since been replaced by a modern structure. The painting is considerably larger than many of Monet's works of the early 1870s, yet it retains the sketch-like qualities of his smaller, informal compositions. The handling of the paint is bold and rapid, and the broken brushwork is used to great effect in the rippling water in the foreground. While the colour scheme is generally muted and harmonious, the dominant greys and browns are enlivened by touches of brighter colour in the sailing-boats and their reflections.

8   Autumn Effect at Argenteuil

Oil on canvas, 56 × 75 cm
Signed and dated: 1873

London, Courtauld Institute Galleries
(The Samuel Courtauld Trust)

Apparently painted from his floating studio, this picture shows the town of Argenteuil in the background, looking upstream across a side branch of the River Seine, the Petit Bras, which encircles the Ile Marante, seen on the left. This inlet was a mooring place for boats too large to be left on the main stretch of the river, but Monet shows a deserted and almost timeless scene, with the view of the town dominated by the church steeple.

The line of the horizon divides the canvas. The mass of trees above the water-line is distinguished from their reflections by a change in the thickness of the paint. The details of the forms are obliterated in favour of an emphasis on the total effect, and on the vivid contrast between the oranges and yellows of the trees, and the blue of water and sky. On the extreme right, a number of parallel lines indicate that Monet scraped away some of the paint layers with the handle of a brush.

9 Woman seated on a Bench

Oil on canvas, 73.7 × 55.9 cm
Signed
About 1874

London, Tate Gallery

Monet's work of the 1870s was dominated by landscape and urban subjects. However, he retained an interest in the human figure, and often painted his family in informal domestic settings.

By tradition, the sitter for this work was a professional model who also posed for several other artists, including Degas. It is painted with a freedom that is exceptional even for Monet. In the background, the ribbons of paint seem to take on a life of their own, while in other areas, such as the dress, Monet uses a form of painterly shorthand. The gaze of the model, who stares directly and inquisitively at the spectator, adds to the spontaneity of the image.

Aspects of the style are similar to the work of Monet's friend Edouard Manet, and this painting may have been executed when the two artists were working together at Argenteuil in 1874.

10 Snow Scene at Argenteuil

Oil on canvas, 71 × 91.5 cm
Signed
1875

Private Collection

This view of Argenteuil calls to mind paintings by Corot: a road recedes in perspective, framed on either side by trees, while small figures give the scene a sense of scale and human presence. Monet was fascinated by the effects of light and colour in snowy scenes, and here the entire landscape is white and blue, with dark touches suggesting the ruts made by a passing coach in the middle of the road, and the rough fence and wall on either side.

Monet wished to capture the atmosphere of the whole scene rather than showing any part in precise detail. The houses in the background are barely indicated, while the figures are suggested simply by a few coloured marks.

11 The Gare St-Lazare

Oil on canvas, 54.3 × 73.6 cm
Signed
1877

London, National Gallery

Monet painted twelve views of the Gare St-Lazare early in
1877. Made within the station and beside the tracks outside
it, they share a preoccupation with the pictorial theme of
smoke. They were probably finished on the spot, but,
unlike later series paintings such as the *Grainstacks* (see
Plate 16), they were not reworked as a group. Seven of the
paintings were shown at the third Impressionist exhibition
in 1877, but it is not certain whether this was one of them.

Monet set up his easel at the terminus of one of the
main lines looking along the *quais* and tracks towards the
Pont de l'Europe in the middle distance. Two locomotives
make steam, while a crowd of passengers wait to board.

The critic Georges Rivière commented on the group of
paintings in 1877: 'These paintings are amazingly varied,
despite the monotony and aridity of the subject. In them,
more than anywhere else, can be seen that skill in
arrangement, that organisation of the canvas, that is one of
the main qualities of Monet's work.'

12 Lavacourt under Snow

Oil on canvas, 59.7 × 80.6 cm
Signed and dated: 1881

London, National Gallery

This is a view of Lavacourt, a hamlet on the opposite side
of the Seine from Vétheuil, where Monet lived from 1878
until 1881.

It was an unsettled time for Monet and his move to
Vétheuil, some sixty kilometres from Paris, marked the
beginning of a period of isolation from his fellow
Impressionists. However, this picture illustrates the
growing assurance of his technique. The paint is applied in
flurries across the canvas, skilfully evoking the thick layers
of snow. The most remarkable feature of the work is the
strident colour. Using a small number of pigments, Monet
creates forceful contrasts and oppositions of colour to
render the play of light across the blanket of snow.

The snow effect demonstrates Monet's developing
interest in extremes of weather. The severe winter of
1879–80, and the dramatic thaw, inspired some of his most
memorable works. Although this canvas bears the date of
1881, it probably dates from several years earlier. The artist
frequently added dates to his pictures long after their
completion and his dating was often inaccurate.

13 Vase of Flowers

Oil on canvas, 100.4 × 81.8 cm
Signed
About 1881–2

London, Courtauld Institute Galleries
(The Samuel Courtauld Trust)

This lavish display of wild mallow is one of a group of still lifes Monet painted between 1878 and 1882, the only period in his career that he concentrated extensively on this type of painting. Monet experienced difficulties in completing such a large still life, and did not sell it at the time of its execution: photographs show it still hanging in his house at Giverny around 1920.

The blooms lack definition, and the effect is one of deceptive simplicity, unlike Monet's more formally arranged still lifes in the tradition of Chardin, or the carefully observed group of fruits of the late 1860s (Plate 2). The line of the table-top is imprecise, and the vase and flower arrangement tilt to the left.

14 Antibes

Oil on canvas, 65.5 × 92.4 cm
Signed and dated: 1888

London, Courtauld Institute Galleries
(The Samuel Courtauld Trust)

Monet was in Antibes from February until May 1888. This painting shows the view south-west from the Cap d'Antibes across the Golfe Juan, with the Montagnes de l'Estérel in the background. The town of Cannes is just out of sight on the right-hand side of the bay. Antibes was becoming a place favoured by tourists at this time, and Monet's paintings of such sites were beginning to attract buyers. He showed ten paintings of Antibes at the Montmartre gallery of Boussod and Valadon run by Theo van Gogh, Vincent's brother, in June 1888.

Monet found capturing the intensity of southern light and colour challenging. He wrote to his Impressionist colleague Berthe Morisot: 'It's so difficult, so tender and so delicate, while I'm so inclined to brutality.' He described the sky as so blue that one 'swims' in it, and felt that the light was so brilliant that to render it one would need gold and gemstones. But finally he was satisfied with his efforts, and wrote to Alice Hoschedé: 'What I bring back from here will be sweetness itself, white, pink, blue, all of it enveloped in this fairytale-like air.'

15   Study of Rocks: The Creuse (Le Bloc)

Oil on canvas, 72.4 × 91.4 cm
Signed and dated: 1889

HM Queen Elizabeth, The Queen Mother

Monet joined the critic Gustave Geffroy and two of his friends on an excursion to the Creuse Valley, in the Massif Central in central France, in the summer of 1889. The rugged landscape of the Creuse was sparsely populated but had long attracted painters, and Monet quickly succumbed to what he described as the 'awesome wildness' of the place. He painted twenty-four canvases on this campaign, ten depicting the convergence of the Petit Creuse and Grand Creuse rivers, and showed at least fourteen of them in a joint exhibition with Auguste Rodin at Georges Petit's gallery in June 1889.

The painting is sombre and severe, and Monet himself was startled by the impact of the group of Creuse views. 'In looking at my series, I was terrified to find them so sombre. It is going to be a lugubrious series.' The painting shows the rock that rises above the point of convergence of the rivers. It seems almost to burst out of the dimensions of the canvas, its strength and weight dwarfing the ragged line of trees on the horizon.

16 Grainstack (Sunset: Winter)

Oil on canvas, 64.8 × 92.1 cm
Signed and dated: 1891

Private Collection

Monet began a series of paintings of grainstacks in 1888, and resumed work on it in the winter of 1890–1. By February 1891, there were twenty-five canvases, of different dimensions, all with simple compositions, consisting of one or two stacks in a field, with houses set against a line of background hills. Fifteen of the paintings were exhibited to great acclaim by the dealer Durand-Ruel in Paris in May 1891. They quickly established Monet's reputation with American buyers, who clamoured to buy the *Grainstacks*.

Positioned against the setting sun, the stack in this painting is fiery in colour, the earth surrounding it indicated by brilliant yellows, blues and pinks. The application of paint is densely layered. The conical top of the thatched stack meets the horizon line in a strongly geometric manner, and the apparent simplicity of the arrangement belies the care and craft Monet applied to this painting. The critic Camille Mauclair, often hostile, saw here 'a great painter…[producing] a surety of execution that is almost mathematical.'

17 Poplars on the Epte

Oil on canvas, 92.4 × 73.7 cm
Signed and dated: 1890

London, Tate Gallery

In June 1891, Monet collaborated with a local timber merchant in order to purchase the land on which these poplars grew. They stood on the banks of the Epte, two kilometres south of Monet's home at Giverny, and were planted at regular intervals, just over two metres apart.

Monet painted a series of *Poplars*, stressing the decorative harmony of the trees. He chose a vantage point for this painting where the River Epte made an S-curve, so that we see a screen of trees in the foreground and a receding group beyond. The slender dark trunks of the poplars seem to march across the vibrant blue sky. The painting is not as heavily worked as many in the series, suggesting that Monet had indicated the main elements of the scene but had not taken the canvas to the point of finish seen, for example, in the *Grainstack* (Plate 16).

Although the painting bears a date of 1890, all Monet's other pictures of this view are dated 1891 or undated, so the date on this one seems to be a mistake.

18 The Seine at Port-Villez

Oil on canvas, 65.4 × 100.3 cm
Signed and dated: 1885

London, Tate Gallery

Monet painted the Seine at Port-Villez, close to Giverny, on several occasions. In this picture the gently curving hillside and a group of trees combine with their reflections in a simple, almost abstract composition. The design, with its strong sense of two-dimensional pattern, recalls Monet's enthusiasm for Japanese art. However, the effect of mist and the soft, diffuse light suggest an affinity with Corot, whom Monet would later describe as the 'greatest landscape painter'. In the 1890s, Monet became especially enthusiastic about the qualities of poetry and harmony in Corot's work. As in the art of his predecessor, the subdued, almost monochromatic colour and the soft brushwork contribute to a mood of silent reverie.

Although it is dated 1885, this picture almost certainly dates from 1894. Monet may have added the incorrect date by mistake when he sold the picture to the dealer Durand-Ruel in 1911.

19 Flood Waters

Oil on canvas, 71 × 91.5 cm
Stamped
1896

London, National Gallery

After a prolonged period of rainfall in September and October of 1896, the River Epte flooded the fields near Monet's home at Giverny. In a letter to his dealer, Durand-Ruel, Monet complained that the bad weather had left him stranded in Giverny and had prevented him from visiting Paris. This work was painted during that autumn flood. A row of ordinary willow trees bordering a field was transformed into an unusual subject. Surrounded by water, the dark trunks and sinewy branches are silhouetted against the pale greys of the flood.

The painting seems unfinished and was presumably painted in haste in front of the subject. A signed and dated version of this composition is now in a private collection. The latter is more fully developed and may have been painted in the studio, using the National Gallery painting as a sketch.

20 The Water-Lily Pond

Oil on canvas, 88.3 × 93.1 cm
Signed and dated: 1899

London, National Gallery

In 1890 Monet bought the house he had rented in Giverny
since 1883, and in 1893 acquired the land on the other side
of the road and railway tracks that bordered the property.
He announced his intention of diverting the River Epte
with a system of sluices to construct something 'for the
pleasure of the eye and also for motifs to paint'.

The resulting pond was crossed by the Japanese
footbridge represented here, and filled with water-lilies.
The plantings of this garden took several years to mature,
and it was not until 1899 that Monet began to paint it. In
this year, he produced a series of eighteen views of the
pond and footbridge.

The curve of the bridge spans the canvas, a man-made
accent in the profusion of rich green foliage of the pond
and its surrounds. The delicate pinks of the water-lilies on
the surface of the water are suggested by dense encrustations
of paint. In the extreme foreground, the reflection of the
footbridge appears in a small area where the surface of the
water is clear.

21 Water-Lilies, Sunset

Oil on canvas, 73 × 92 cm
Signed
1907–8

Private Collection

In this picture, which probably dates from 1907–8, Monet adopted one of his favoured compositional formats. The lily-pads seem to drift across the flat surface of the picture, but the bank in the foreground helps to anchor the composition and to allow a more traditional feeling of depth and space to emerge. The sunset reflected in the pond adds a note of gentle melancholy which sometimes pervades the water-lily paintings.

Today, Monet's garden at Giverny is a popular tourist attraction. As the crowds move slowly along the banks of the pond or gather on the Japanese bridge, it is often difficult to imagine the serenity that Monet must have enjoyed in his own private environment. As one of his contemporaries noted, 'as soon as you push the little entrance gate on the main street of Giverny you think, in almost all seasons, that you are entering a paradise'.

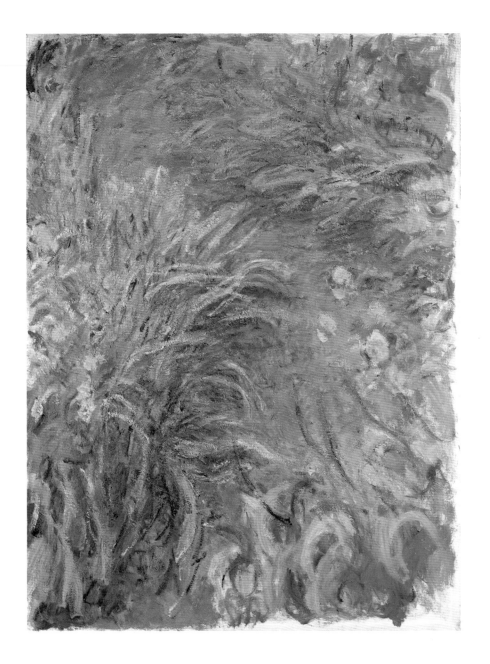

22 Irises

Oil on canvas, 200.7 × 149.9 cm
About 1914–17

London, National Gallery

'Perhaps it was because of flowers that I became a painter',
Monet said towards the end of his life. The garden that he
created at Giverny was in some sense a work of art with its
rows of blossoms reflecting sunlight in an opulent display
of colour and texture. In this enclosed world, Monet was
able to shape and harness the forces of nature, closing the
gap between reality and art.

Monet grew irises along the banks of his pond at
Giverny. The unusual perspective of this view suggests that
he may have been looking down on the flowers, perhaps
from the Japanese bridge. The curve of a winding path
articulates the composition and divides the plants into
clusters across the picture surface.

This canvas is the same height as Monet's largest
water-lily paintings, but although it probably dates from
around 1914–17, it does not seem to have been conceived
as part of this series.

23 Water-Lilies

Oil on canvas, 148.5 × 164 cm
Stamped
1917

Private Collection

In this large canvas, Monet depicts the water-lilies as almost abstract shapes on the surface of the dark pond. Unseen trees on the bank are reflected in the water, making a dense background to the circular lily-pads, which appear to float free of the canvas. The water-lilies in the foreground are indicated by calligraphy-like marks, which stress the two-dimensional surface of the canvas. In these late works, there is a move away from subject matter and a stress on mood and decoration. It was such work which led the influential American critic Clement Greenberg to declare that the late works of Monet are more radical than the work of the Dutch De Stijl painter Piet Mondrian: '[Mondrian's painting] is more traditional in its color, as well as in its subservience to the frame, than the last paintings of Monet are.' Greenberg also stressed the links between such late works of Monet and the generation of American painters of the 1950s such as Rothko, Still and Newman: 'Late Impressionism was the precedent here, and as in the late Monet, the suppression of value contrasts created a new kind of openness. The picture no longer divided itself into shapes or even patches, but into zones and areas and fields of color.'

24 Water-Lilies

Oil on canvas, 101.6 × 200.66 cm
Stamped
About 1917–19

Private Collection

Monet's larger water-lily paintings were produced in the studio, although he used smaller works, which had been painted outdoors, for reference. His paintings were often the result of protracted labour and the effort to record endlessly shifting nuances of light and colour sometimes drove him to distraction. He claimed he was 'constantly haunted by what he was trying to realize' and declared that 'painting is so difficult and torturing'.

In this work, painted in about 1917–19, the richly textured, granular surface bears witness to the artist's repeated reworkings as he sought to fix the most transitory of effects. Yet the deft movements of his brush and the delicacy of his colours disguise any anxieties that may have gone into the production of such a large work. Monet closes in on the surface of the pond, concentrating on the counterpoint between the floating lily-pads and the ethereal reflections of trees and sky. According to Monet, it was the ever-changing appearance of the 'mirror of water' which was the essence of this subject.

25 Water-Lilies

Oil on canvas, 200.7 × 426.7 cm
Stamped
After 1916

London, National Gallery

In 1914, at the instigation of his friend the statesman Georges Clemenceau, Monet began work on a series of large-scale paintings of water-lilies, which he planned to present to the French nation. Two years later, he moved into a specially constructed studio at Giverny which could accommodate his vast canvases. To house these murals, two rooms were built to Monet's design in the Orangerie in Paris, and the works were eventually installed in 1927, the year after the artist's death. This picture is one of a number of canvases which were evolved alongside the scheme for the Orangerie, but which were not included in the final installation. The cheerful yellows and pale greens are quite different from the more resonant blues and purples which predominate in the Orangerie paintings.

In some respects, these monumental canvases represent the culmination of Monet's search to find equivalents in paint for elusive sensations of nature. Surrounding the spectator, the swirling patterns of colour can easily lose all definition. Yet the thickly applied paint resists abstraction and our eyes adjust to find the surface of the pond receding into depth, punctuated by floating lily-pads. The reflections of clouds and sky help to evoke a sense of limitless space.

CLAUDE MONET – A CHRONOLOGY

1840   Born 14 November, rue Laffitte, Paris.

1845   The Monet family moves to Le Havre.

1850s   Meets Boudin, who encourages him to work out of doors.

1859   Moves to Paris to study painting. Meets Camille Pissarro.

1861   Begins military service in Algeria.

1862   Returns to Le Havre on convalescent leave, and meets Jongkind. Is released from military service and returns to Paris. Enrols in the *atelier* of Charles Gleyre.

1864   Paints along the coast at Honfleur with fellow-artist Bazille.

1866   Exhibits *Woman in a Green Dress (Camille)* at the Salon, where it is well received.

1868   Exhibits five paintings at the International Maritime Exhibition in Le Havre. Wins silver medal.

1870–1   Marries Camille Doncieux. Travels to London and Holland. Returns to Paris in 1871, renting a house in Argenteuil.

1873–4   With Pissarro, Sisley and Renoir, plans a society of artists to exhibit independently of the Salon. The first group exhibition is held in 1874 at Nadar's former photography studio on the boulevard des Capucines. A critic names the group 'Impressionists' after the title of one of Monet's paintings, *Impression: Sunrise*.

1876   Second Impressionist exhibition at Galerie Durand-Ruel. Meets Ernest Hoschedé who commissions Monet to paint large decorative works at Montgeron.

1877   Fellow-artist Caillebotte rents a studio for Monet near the Gare St-Lazare, which Monet depicts in a series of paintings. Showed seven *Gare St-Lazare* paintings at the third Impressionist exhibition.

1878   Takes a house in Vétheuil on the Seine.

1879   Fourth Impressionist exhibition, backed by Caillebotte. Camille dies.

1881   Moves to Poissy near Paris, followed by Alice Hoschedé and her children.

1882   Shows thirty-six paintings at the seventh Impressionist exhibition. Works along the Normandy coast.

1883–4   First one-man exhibition at Galerie Durand-Ruel. Takes a house at Giverny. Also travels to the south of France and, in 1884, to Bordighera, in north Italy.

1885–7   Works extensively at Etretat on the Normandy coast and at Belle-Ile-en-Mer in Brittany.

1888   Paints at Antibes and Juan-les-Pins in the south of France. Begins *Grainstacks* series.

1890   Buys house in Giverny.

1891   Begins *Poplars* series on the banks of the River Epte.

1892   Stays in Rouen and begins painting *Cathedrals* series. Marries Alice Hoschedé, Ernest Hoschedé having died in 1891.

1893   Continues work in Rouen, and buys land near his home in Giverny, which he turns into a water garden.

1894   Visited by Cézanne at Giverny.

1896   Begins *Mornings on the Seine* series.

1899–1901   Works on series of views of the Thames in London

1902   Begins *Water-Lilies* series.

1908   Travels to Venice.

1909   Forty-eight water-lily paintings exhibited at the Galerie Durand-Ruel

1914   Begins series of mural-sized versions of the *Water-Lilies*.

1920   Announcement of Monet's intention to donate twelve large water-lily paintings to the State, to be exhibited in a pavilion in the gardens of the Hôtel Biron (Rodin Museum).

1921   Space in the Orangerie is offered for the *Water-Lilies*.

1923   Operations for cataracts in both eyes.

1926   Dies 5 December, aged eighty-six.

1927   The *Water-Lilies* murals are installed in the Orangerie.